FURRY TAILS

Cats tell tales of their once-famous owners

Written and illustrated

By

Pamela Binns

Index

Whose Cat?	3
Damien Hirst's Cat	7
Tracey's Cat	9
Socks: The Cat At Shaw's Corner	13
A Life Together - Leonardo's Cat	17
Léhar's Cat, Vilja	21
Van Gogh's Cat	25
The Haymarket Cat	27
Van Dyck's Cat	31
Grayson Perry's Cat	35
The Cat Odysseus Left Behind	37
Little Miss M.	41

Whose Cat?

I am Dick Whittington's all black cat -

Remember that!

We set off for London Town,

Where Dick thought he'd claim a crown.

"All the pavements paved with gold",

That was the story we'd been told.

But when we got to Highgate High,

Dick sat down and heaved a sigh.

"Puss," he said, "we must retreat,

No luck in London we will meet."

He no longer wished to roam.

He was all for going home.

All that talk of turning back

I'd have liked his bot to smack!

I was the one who changed his mind -

Saying in London we'd prospects find.

Although gold nuggets we didn't discover

Our startling story is not yet over.

The streets we paced, we were very poor,

We had to beg from door to door.

(A job was very hard to get

Something we must not forget.)

When Dick was working on a boat -

(I did not care for life afloat)

I caught the rats that tarried there -

An answer to the Captain's prayer!

This praise gave Dick his greatest chance

His lifetime prospects to advance.

He climbed fames's ladder, frame by frame,

Lord Mayor of London he became!

Dick is remembered, talked of still,

I changed it all on Highgate Hill.

Those stupid bells didn't make him turn

'Twas my claws behind him, strong and stern.

People thought we were a pair,

He'd steal the limelight, 'twasn't fair.

Dick's a legend …. I'm forgot.

"Only the cat" - that is my lot.

But I was Dick Whittington's famous cat -

Miaow! …. remember that!

Damien Hirst's Cat

I am the cat of Damien Hirst.

He's kept me alive – at least that's a first!

He's planning and plotting, and wants me to die.

What will he do with my corpse when it's high?

In formaldehyde I think I'll be set -

My sleek glossy coat all nasty and wet.

Disgusting I'll smell, and disgusted I'll be,

But there'll be some fool who'll pay to see me.

All studded with diamonds I think I might end,

A present a Prince or a Royal might send.

My pussy-cat powers tell me I must leave

Before his quite horrible spell he can weave

And captures my body, and seizes and rapes

And twists it around into horrible shapes

That the gullible'll buy. I see we must part,

I must leave Damien's service, I still have a heart.

I shall leap on a bus, or perhaps take a train

To somewhere D.H. won't find me again

Tracey's Cat

I am Tracey Emin's cat -

How I wonder what she's at!

I've been with her from the start.

I'm the mainstay of her art.

But things she does, I don't approve,

Makes our friendship far from smooth.

First there was the Unmade Bed,

I think of that, enough's been said:

All that rubbish, puerile waste,

'Twasn't comfy, not my taste;

Not a snuggly sleep for me,

To make it real, I left a flea.

Then there was the famous Tent,

Not an idea from heaven sent.

One by one the lovers named

(Most of them have now been shamed).

Each and every one was trash,

(Most of them were stoned on hash).

To aid the truth I did a pee

Just where everyone could see.

You know she can draw really well -

But then she tries so hard to sell.

All this trifling stuff's a lark -

Helping make her worldly mark.

But if <u>my</u> portrait she would paint

She'd be hailed the R.A.'s Saint.

Socks: The Cat At Shaw's Corner

I am the cat who lives at Shaw's Corner,

Of course, I didn't meet the venerable owner.

But I do know the numerous plays that he wrote -

In fact I have learnt a great many by rote.

In summer the actors come acting his plays,

It's fun to distract them in quite different ways:

I walk-on when required (and quite often when not)

I feel that my presence enhances the plot.

When a prompt line is needed I give a "Miaow!"

An unheralded entrance can be such a wow.

The audience look at me, and not at the cast,

A silence ensues that some minutes can last.

When the actors stand up in an orderly line

I know the applause has been earned and is mine!

Old Shaw is now spinning in his vaulted grave,

But as Cat of the Corner I know how to behave.

I welcome the visitors, show them around,

(And when pooing dig very small holes in the ground.)

Courtesy and kindness to all I have shown -

"The Feline of Destiny" is how I am known.

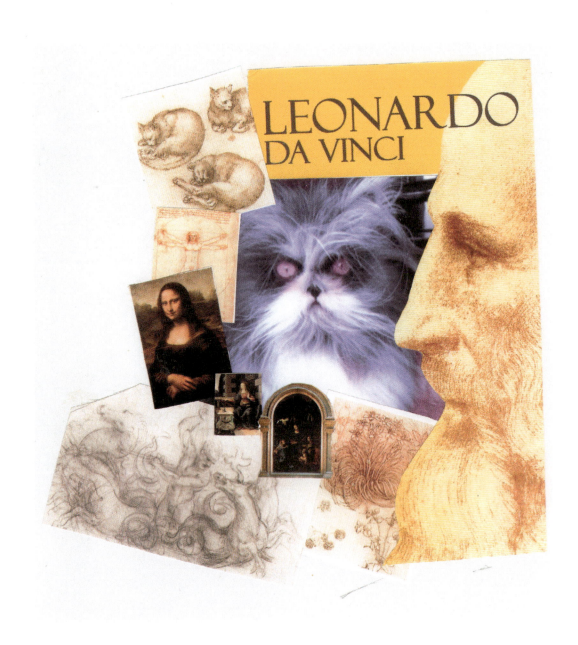

A Life Together – Leonardo's Cat

Leonardo my master, I served him well,

I kept rat numbers down, and the mouses as well.

He drew me quite often, awake or asleep,

And when he was out, at his sketch book I'd peep.

So that's what I look like! My fur with a shine.

No one had a master who painted like mine.

When the strange lady for her portrait she sat,

I played in the corner and rumpled the mat.

"Be still!" my master commanded her, grim,

So she turned her full face to focus on him.

But she'd seen me at play, and gave a half smile,

She was called Gioconda, the name stuck a while.

So she became famous, and my master too,

Though sadly of paintings he left but a few.

He drew violets and acorns, trees of all kind,

The parts of the body, binding heart with the mind.

There were duels and quarrels and lawsuits galore,

So my master toiled day and the nights even more.

He opened up corpses, wielding his knife,

But for me with my master, a wonderful life.

He made horses and armies; and hair became streams,

And he drew what he saw, and for others, their dreams.

The King offered us shelter, we journeyed to France,

Our life there settled, a grace-filled trance.

But his time was numbered, and running out fast.

The King came to visit. That day was his last.

The King kissed him 'goodbye'; and I was alone,

The house by the Loire was no longer my home.

Miaow!

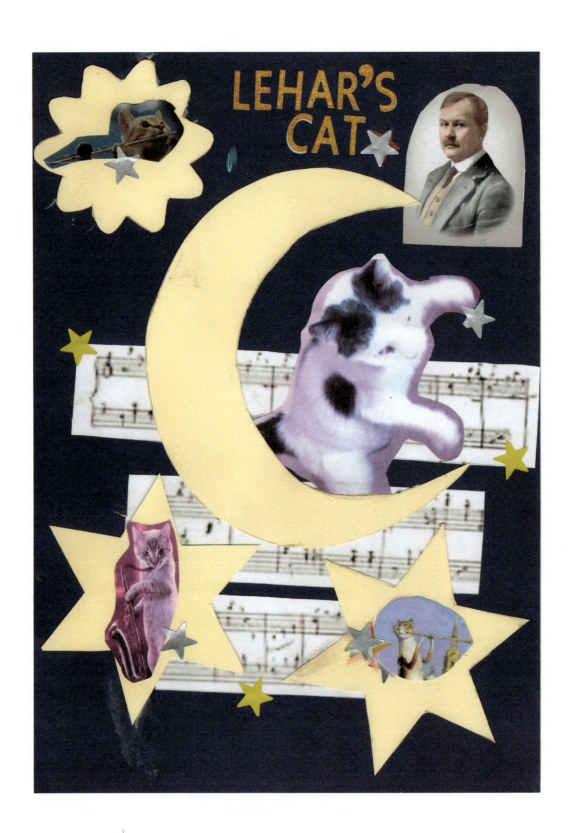

Léhar's Cat, Vilja

My master's name was Franz Léhar,

Formerly bandsman, later a star.

Léhar the bandsman, born and bred

Could never get rid of the tunes in his head.

So he joined the navy to see the sea,

But the earworms continued, he wasn't set free.

He was made to study the violin,

Then told composition was not for him,

So in desperation he joined a band

And toured the cities throughout the land.

He tootled his trombone and marched and marched,

His feet were sore and his throat was parched.

I joined him first at a lodging house,

He picked me up and I purred in his purse.

'Vilja' he called me, from a woodland sprite,

It was then that he really learned to write.

For the tunes went round and round in his head,

"I must jot them down," was what he said.

Waltzes, polkas and dances galore,

Each night he carefully wrote the score.

He had a song he couldn't name -

"Vilja!" he cried, it brought him fame.

This song was to crown the best thing he wrote,

'The Merry Widow' won everyone's vote,

Hundred and thousands of copies were sold;

The song of my name was worth more than gold.

The operetta made my master's name,

And brought Léhar his worldwide fame.

Van Gogh's Cat

I was the Cat of Vincent Van Gogh,

His early years were terribly tough.

He came south to seek the sun,

He really felt his life had begun.

But his beautiful landscapes no one wanted:

Van Gogh was afraid he might be haunted.

His friend Gauguin came to stay,

I hoped they'd peacefully paint all day.

But no, their rows grew worse and worse,

My master believed he was under a curse,

He painted wild sky-scapes with sizzling stars,

He cut off his ear. He was shut behind bars.

To the asylum I could not go.

I walked about in the sleet and the snow.

I was the cat of Vincent Van Gogh,

Who never loved me, or himself, enough.

The Haymarket Cat

I am the Cat of the Haymarket Theatre,

But I do rather more than catch mice by the metre.

I'm the Head Cat when they've all gone home.

Back stage and the circles I freely roam.

I've sat in the wings and watched all the Greats -

Olivier and Jacobi, they were my mates.

When Dame Sybil was here I helped her to knit,

(She fashioned a cardie for my favourite kit.)

When John G. was playing he committed a crime

For something we now wouldn't think worth a dime.

He really was foolish, he went and got caught

And his fame and his honours all counted for naught.

He refused to go on, the curtain was down,

He shivered and shook – for all his renown.

"You're just being silly," whispered Syb. in his ear.

"Go out and face them, you've nothing to fear."

So the curtain was raised and Sir John took the stage,

The audience cheered, it went on for an age,

And Sir John, (how we loved him) a tear on his cheek

Was so moved and so humbled he barely could speak,

And he gave the performance, his finest that week.

The audience attendance shot up to its peak.

At night times I stalk all the ghosts that are here,

I'm a bit of a mystic, rather more of a seer.

And yes, I am fecund, I don't make a sound,

But in seconds the lady cats all come around.

We dance and we play, and the other thing too.

There'll be kittens for Christmas: perhaps one for you?

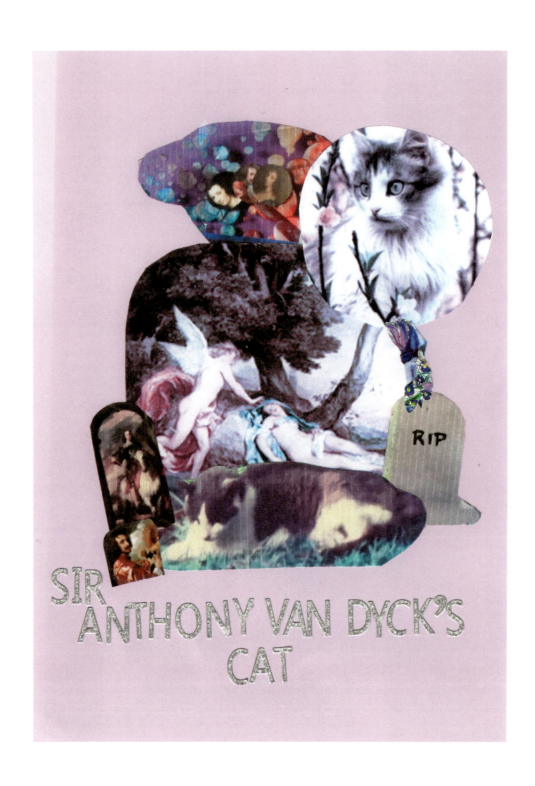

Van Dyck's Cat

I was the Cat of Sir Anthony van Dyck,

And I'll tell you a story that you may not like:

It happened at the very end of his life

When his mistress, Margaret, supplanted his wife.

Altho' by then his affections were waning,

Margaret was jealous, her behaviour quite shaming:

She was modelling for him as Psyche the Goddess

In a blue silk gown that wasn't quite modest.

She suddenly learnt a new mistress he had

Her temper flared up, and she did something bad -

Put her teeth round his finger, attempted to bite!

Poor Sir Anthony had the most terrible fright,

But luckily moved his hand very quickly

(There was only a smear of blood which was sickly.)

He assured her he loved her, that she was his own,

(How quickly her teeth could have gnawed through his bone!)

On Eros' profile he put his own face,

For my master was running, and losing, a race

Against the Great Reaper. Death had come calling

Whom none can defeat, nor bribe into stalling.

But in the great painting, you'll see them together

Eros and Psyche entwined there for ever.

His right hand outstretched, that might have been lost

His whole career ended, at such a great cost.

I crept to his graveside, I mewed and I cried,

Though nothing could alter: my master had died.

But his paintings remain, for the great and the glory

And now I, poor pussy, have told you his story.

Grayson Perry's Cat

I am Grayson Perry's Cat:

Nothing very odd in that -

Except – I think I am a dog,

(I always use the puppy's bog.)

I begged a collar and a lead,

And go for walks, and get up speed.

I leap the fences in a bound,

(Less like a feline, more a hound.)

All very fine if I were doggie,

But truth to tell, I am a moggie.

PINTORICCHIO

The Cat Odysseus Left Behind

I am the Cat left behind by Odysseus,

Who trusted me to keep guard on his missus.

Penelope wove, and I sat by her loom,

(With all the men gone, it was quiet in the room.)

Then the Suitors arrived, they jostled and jeered,

They all wanted to wed her, it was frightening and weird.

"When my tapestry's finished, one of you I will wed,"

Replied Penelope calmly. That's what she said.

But to keep to her word and avoid getting hitched

Up all night sat Penelope, and her wool work unstitched.

The suitors returned, all ready to bed,

But the work not completed, not one could she wed.

They all ran amok, and smashed trophies and all

The treasures and heirlooms that were kept in the hall.

Odysseus came home. He was heavily disguised.

He found ruin and plunder in all that he'd prized.

He'd kept his bow hidden, his options were narrow

To win back his wife with just the one arrow.

To the Suitors Odysseus offered a challenge:

(He was furious they'd tried to break up his marriage.)

Twelve hoops he hung for their arrows to pass

As swiftly and surely as reflections in glass.

He knew that they could not. He knew that his bow

Could loosen an arrow through twelve in a row

And that's how it was. The Suitors all failed,

And Odysseus as champion was acknowledged and hailed.

Then Odysseus turned killer: Suitors axed one by one,

And I, who was watching, saw justice was done.

So Penelope and Odysseus once more were wed,

And I watched them as lovingly they went to bed.

And if you should doubt that this Cat is not me

There's the painting in the National Gall-ry.

                Miaow!

Little Miss M.

Little Miss M. lived alone with her cat

Up fifty stairs in a single room flat.

It was dusty and dirty and all smelt of mould,

There was no form of heating, and so it was cold.

Little Miss M. of her cat was so fond -

Affection between them an unbroken bond.

How Little Miss M. longed for stripes and some fur,

To be like her friend, and speak with a purr.

The cat cuddled closer, and purred even more,

And lovingly touched her old face with a paw.

Then gently licked her with rough little tongue:

Miss M. was remembering when she was young

Those times that were wreathed in a bright golden haze

Of sun-filled happiness, dancing the days.

Unlike the present, where she had grown old,

And all was in darkness, and bitterly cold.

For now both her feet had quite turned to ice,

And the comfort the cat gave could hardly suffice.

The catkin continued her comforting purr:

"I wish I was wearing your all-over fur."

A strange gurgling sound came into her throat:

Coughing and carolling, all on one note.

Little Miss M. was breathing so fast -

Little Miss M. was purring at last!

She gave a sigh. Was happy. Was gone.

The cat was left in the room alone.

Printed in Great Britain
by Amazon

29648159R00027